Poetry Through a Rearview Mirror

Reflections on love, loss and legacy

Gordon J. Mitchell

Dedication

To Dylan Thomas: "Do not go gentle into that good night".

Foreword

This collection reflects a poetic journey taken by me over the past several years. Mine is not a heroic poetry, nor a poetry of historical sweep, but rather a poetry of joy, love and reflection. It speaks to the nature of sandcastles and rainbows, to ghosts that still linger in a famous Parisian café, and to when old age made spectators of us all.

You are invited to come along on this journey, starting with the vibrancy of childhood and the wisdom of grandchildren to the quiet struggles of lingering grief and mortality, and finally towards what reflections may lie ahead in a rearview mirror.

These poems are the songs between moments. Listen gently.

About the Author

Gordon J. Mitchell is a Montreal-born poet and educator whose work draws from decades of observing the shifting landscapes of expectation and experience. His writing blends lyrical storytelling with deep thought, often informing everyday experiences such as café tables, rainbows and riverbanks with the gravity of emotional conflict and resolution. In his poems, the past is never quite past, and even fleeting moments carry the echoes of memory. Gordon's poetry has been praised for its emotional clarity, rich imagery and gently humorous soul.

Table of Contents

I. The Delights of Childhood

Childhood, Wonder & Discovery

The journey begins where dew glistens on new-boy feet and imagination reigns in sandcastles by the sea.

These poems capture the joys of youth on early April mornings, the poignancy of summers before turning Sweet Sixteen, and the everlasting sweetness of giant poppy seed cookies.

Whether chasing rainbows or the nostalgia of lost summers, these poems trace the arc of childhood, reminding us that joy is a precious gift we carry forward.

April Boys

A poem about the joy of being a boy in April

April mornings
drip-dropped
winter drip-dropped
down the drain
through the eaves trough
down the lane
along the gutter
quick with rain
where we sailed
through puddles
on pirate seas.

April mornings
drip-dropped
we doffed our winter boots
and ran on new boy feet
along the April streets
the sun flashed warm
across our backs
as it dripped away
the snowplow tracks
and turned the driveways
witch-house black.

April mornings
drip-dropped
snow forts dripping
down the drain

like sandcastles
washed away by rain
we traded mitts and hats
for baseball bats
and raced on bikes
along the lanes.

April mornings
drip-dropped
spring crept slowly
'neath the windowsills
and poked up through
the playground hills
where we wrestled
in the near-May sand
and dug to China
with shovel hands.

April mornings
drip-dropped
April's slipping
down the drain
through the eaves trough
along the lane.
March has passed
May's yet to come
but those April boys
are now all undone.

Giant Poppy Seed Cookies

A poem about youthful memories of a special treat

Beyond these jagged frontier peaks
thrust bold up through the BC cloud
like Pacific seas struck in stone
I see my soft Laurentian hills.

Those gentle childhood summer hills
where we first held life in trembling hands
like the quivering beat of a palmed bird
in thick stands of silver birch and spruce.

The first out the screen door morning dew
was cool moist between our bare-boy feet
as we ran along Leblanc's hay-cut fields
with Mama calling for socks and shoes.

"Shawbridge Bakery! Shawbridge Bakery!"
the truck blared each morning quarter to eight
as cottage wives buzzed with screen porch gossip
and pulled dollar bills from house coat pockets.

Above the sweet smell of new morning bread
they clutched buns and bagels in cigarette fingers
to serve up with coffee on mid-morning tables
and chat about politics and crooning singers.

As we kids dashed along the afternoon banks
of the Rivière du Nord, playing steal-the-flag
pulling tall bullrushes from the late-day clay
to light with wood matches for midnight parades.

Along the flagstone path between little post houses
beside bonfires dancing with ghosts and goblins
we waited for Mama with giant poppy seed cookies
then it was off to sleep in knotty pine bedrooms.

Did the rain fall more gently on those soft summer hills
as it washed away the after-midnight, can't sleep heat
between tossed-off blankets and sweat-slicked sheets
where we dreamed merrily of giant poppy seed cookies?

The Nature of Sandcastles

A poem about the true nature of sandcastles

It was really and truly something grand
shaped by my boy's very own hands
a masterpiece in sand, you might say
with high round turrets, a deep moat
and a fine stockade, as Sacha proclaimed
it would surely keep all the bad guys away.

I offered to help him complete his castle
help him win some make-believe battles
all the time fearing that the evening tide
would wash it clean away without a trace
and cast dark shadows across his face.

We worked on the sandcastle all that day
it was quite something to behold if I do say
as make believe knights on Arabian stallions
we fought off pirates, saved poor damsels
and found chests of gold in sunken galleons.

But when we returned the following day
the castle was gone, washed back to the sea
Sacha was terribly upset as you might expect
I could feel the pain stealing away his joy
but what can you say to a ten year-old boy.

In the following days, we rebuilt his castle
rekindled his wonder, won some more battles
but soon vacation was done, we had to move on
so we packed up our stuff and started for home
and as I peered at Sacha in the back of the van
he seemed less like a boy but not yet a man.

Such is the nature of sandcastles.

Before We All Turned Sweet Sixteen

A poem about leaving childhood summers behind

Summer mornings picking dandelions
above the lush of dew-moist grass
high-pitched whirr of mower engines
echoing down a lazy morning path
whirl of insects boisterously buzzing
high above a carpet of golf course green
this is how we spent our last summer
before we all turned Sweet Sixteen.

Glare of sun on white-bleached sheets
billowing in the mid-morning breeze
sear of hot dogs and sizzling burgers
loudly grilling on black lunchtime grills
children dripping ice cream sundaes
over the broiling afternoon streets
these lasting pictures formed our lives
before we all turned Sweet Sixteen.

Soft touch of bright yellow sunflowers
turning their heads in the dusky lanes
pungent tang of red-ripe raspberries
growing beside a twisting sunset road
hum of hummingbirds hovering above
a dark golden crown of evergreens
these were the moments of our lives
before we all turned Sweet Sixteen.

Evening black along flagstone paths
leading up to knotty pine houses
prickly taste of cold Cott Orange soda
sweet and bitter, and oh so very fine
yells of children playing steal-the-flag
with flaming bullrushes for each team
then midnight sleep of dog-tired children
before we all turned Sweet Sixteen.

Will we miss those sweet summer days
will we recall them at all, it's hard to say?
But I know they will reappear in rhyme
in the wonderous look in our kiddos' eyes
as we sing them to sleep in their own time
with tales of how we spent our last summer
before we all turned Sweet Sixteen.

The Wonder of Rainbows

A poem about the wonder of rainbows in a three-year old's eyes

We saw a magnificent rainbow on Edouard's third birthday
my grandson looked up in silent awe at its perfect sweep
his young eyes reflecting the grandeur of its ever rising arch
as it emerged from somewhere beyond the ridge of horizon
and exploded in bold strokes of cobalt, indigo and ruby red.

Edouard stared up and asked a typical young boy question
"Who made that beautiful rainbow in the sky, Mémé?"
What can you tell a three-year old boy about rainbows?

He asked if I had placed it there myself, his mouth agape
as he watched its faultless flight across the twilight sky.
Could it turn downwards and crash into our house?

He begged me to carry him to where it rose from the earth
as if he needed to touch it with his outstretched fingers
or grasp its celestial splendor in his outstretched hands.

I worried how to answer without sweeping the wonder
from his young eyes or forever shutting his tiny fingers
as they slowly traced the rainbow against the setting sun.

I finally asked who *he* thought had made the rainbow
he searched the ground with that shy downward glance
of a child who is unsure about exactly how to reply.

Then he lifted his head and simply said "It's a birthday gift
from you and grandma", placing his hand back in mine.

I swallowed my amazement, then assured him he was right
as we walked back to bed beneath the glow of starlit night.

II. Love & Loss at Any Age

Love Found, Lost & Remembered

The journey continues with love discovered, lost and remembered.

Whether it is pressed between the pages of a book, reflected in a moonlit memory or whispered across a hospice table, these poems illuminate the different faces of love, always with tenderness and often with pain.

Whether illuminating a forgotten Champagne kiss, the grandfather who sees his beloved descending a winding stair or the delicious feeling of nothingness on a warm cottage hill, these poems speak of love that survives absence and enlightens the present.

A Pressed Sunflower

A poem about lost love and flower pressing

For you, I'll free this flower from the book
once more it will beat in my open palm
recalling your embrace
in its slow and perfect
dance.

For you, I'll let this flower bloom
again it will turn towards the sun
exploding in my trembling hands
like an ochre storm
disinterred.

For you, I'll have a gentle rain
wet these parched and brittle leaves
unfolding your last caress
to bloom once more
upon my cheek.

For you, I'll tear this flower from the earth
again I'll press it between the pages
of an unturned book
searching for the sun
always.

Lady in the Mirror

A poem about a particular lady who vanishes down a hall

What is left
when the morning breeze
scatters your shadow
over a cold and polished floor?

When the night has vanished
like a plume of smoke
beneath the window sash
into indifference?

Night steals your veil in its flight
leaving the cold grey dawn
to swallow up your charms
with geometry.

It sweeps your touch from my brow
and your likeness from the mirror
leaving the memory of your kiss
that moonlight made so fair.

Who will fill the mirror now
without your portrait in the night?
Empty in the cold morning light
it stares back accusingly:

"Did she glance at me at all
letting down her chestnut hair?
Or were you simply dreaming
did darkness charm your eyes?"

Morning speaks only lies
in its unforgiving light
belying the curve of your thigh
as you vanished down the hall
it encloses you in poetry
and denies your fall.

What Is It All About?

A poem about how certain questions haunt you in older age

What is it all about?

Was it all about *finding* love at 73
an old man clutching a bent cane
walking along an uncharted beach
with the press of a new love's hand
making little circles in the warming sand?

Or was it all about *recalling* love at 73
the feel of a once-tanned arm
on a once-young summer's eve
fingers that caress a smooth brow
at some forgotten hour of the night?

Or was it all about *regretting* love at 73
lamenting the empty morning rooms
the gloom that obscures the heart
does it really beat more slowly now
ensnarled within a trap of self-doubt?

Or is it really about *rejoicing* in love at 73
the love in a new granddaughter's eyes
running expectedly into your embrace
as she settles contentedly into your lap
is this the meaning of finding grace?

Love of 40 Years

A poem about an incredible lady

He sits
across the hospice table from his love of 40 years
looks in her now rheumy eyes and sees the girl
running barefoot along a Laurentian river bank
the notes of her girlish laugh echoing in the pines.

He studies
the nettled skin wrapping her arthritic fingers
recalls the caution with which they sought him
on rue Dornal when she was still a little shy
and he was transfixed by the light in her eyes.

He marvels
at the memory of her once all embracing voice
so content to place his world within its strength
it echoes now in the corners of his memory
a departed heart that bound them all as one.

He recalls
her selfless love cherishing their little ones
the way she cradled each of them to her breast
until they were ready to soar bold and free
on the rising swell of her ever-generous heart.

He cries
across the hospice table from his love of 40 years
the memory of her is darkening in the fading light
he can barely recall the notes of her girlish laugh
they have sunk too quickly into the gathering night.

Champagne Kiss

A poem about memory, dancing and Krug champagne

While they wait for closing time
his slow hand re-lights
the chewed stub
of a dime-store cigar
while she measures the day's take
by the length of shadow
upon her husband's face.

He watches another February night
steal darkly across
her once fair brow
but she recalls the sparkling sting
of the chilled Krug champagne
tart and quick upon his lips
on their first anniversary kiss.

They went dancing at the Astoria
sure of foot he danced her
across the mirror ball floor
to the tunes of Miller and Shaw
then back to the walk-up flat
to crack open the Krug
and greet the dawn as one.

They will close early tonight
it is their golden anniversary
and they will celebrate
in grand style again
at that new special place
with chicken and potatoes
and sweet Concord Grape.

Later, he will kiss her tenderly
before he nods off to sleep
she will taste the wine again
now thick and sweet
upon his unspeaking lips
and recall the sparkling sting
of their first Champagne kiss.

Passion Play in the Sky

A poem about a small town girl with galaxies in her eyes

As she looks down the little street
   of terraced houses
   their windows bleeding thin light
   onto the scrabble street
   the girl in the loose summer
   dress stands still and solitary
   as galaxies of unimagined colour
   burst silently all about.

Are her eyes fixed downwards
to the dead end of the street
or does she look up and see a
thousand forbidden dreams
dancing for her at last in the
impossibly violent purple sky?
Will they carry her heavenward
on swirling wings of light?

She has always been a prisoner carved in stone
an incomplete statue with uncut eyes and heart
from when she could crawl she needed to soar
above the little houses and habits of her days
to see what lay on the far side of a million stars
as her dreams grew as tumulus as the sky above.

Now she looks up at a thousand forbidden stars
hears the promises of that celestial symphony
and tastes the exotic swirls of an unbounded sky
she feels the heat in the arms of requited lovers
touches the rough animal hide of lawless galaxies
and basks in the brilliance of a thousand suns.

Yes, her time to touch the purple sky has come
she soars above the gray of the terraced houses
rises up on hot air currents of awakening dreams
she bids farewell to the faintness of her sighs
and joins the unimagined passion play in the sky.

Warm Cottage Hills

A poem about the delicious feeling of nothingness

Do you recall
when summer took us
from this place
to one beyond necessity?

Beneath those warm cottage hills
green and lush
with new June grass
we first wept.

I recall your eyes
full and clear and fixed
in a delicate immobility
upon my face.

Was it you
who held your breath
or did time skip a beat
and leave us sleeping?

I see your sweet tears now
fall gently across my brow
freedom at last
the delicious feeling of nothingness.

Zaida

A poem about endearing love even in a retirement home

Zaida sleeps in the corner chair
with her picture by his side
Sophie descending a winding stair
all radiant in black silk and lace
a wedding smile upon her face
almost monumental!

His fingers wrap tightly around
the hook of a rosewood cane
as he sits in the corner chair
his unseeing eyes beyond care
now rheumy and closed by time
still see her sweet beguiling smile.

Though he has held his children's
children to his breast
it is the simple tenderness
of their first wedding day caress
that falls gently down upon him
like ash scattered over time.

They feed him and wash him
and say "He has lost his mind."
he is beyond consequence now
beyond time.

He babbles on about stocks and bonds
and taking the streetcar up to Pine
and they feed him and wash him
and say "He has lost his mind."

But today he is quite aware
rolling tall tales off his tongue
as if we were still quite young
and gathered expectedly at his feet.

Yarns about his railway days
larger than life, longer than time
when he worked as head conductor
on the old CPR transcontinental line.

Stories about his famous passengers
Mackenzie King and Louis St. Laurent
and the wolf call of the steam whistle
across the endless prairie miles.

But suddenly his lips start to tremble
as he turns with an uncertain sigh
touching the portrait beside his chair
"Is that you coming down the stair?"

Now he is gripping the cane so tight
that his fingers are turning bone white
"Is that you coming down the stair?"
as he drops his head back to sleep.

"Zaida, Zaida, where are you now?
I can't see beyond your silent brow
has sleep unveiled a better place
are you there now in her embrace?"

III. Time As Enabler & Thief

Selfhood, Reflection & Aging

These poems reveal the torment of a city changing too fast, the empty shell of a proud man made a spectator by time and the regret of a newspaper vendor whose livelihood has been swept away in the name of progress.

They offer up moments of summers past and a café that was definitely patronized by some very interesting characters.

In searching for meaning in the everyday, they reveal time as both enabler and thief.

When Time Made Spectators of Us All

A poem about how time makes spectators of us all

I visit my dear Zaida whenever I can
he was once quite a prince of a man
a real *mensch*, a someone who cared
but now he just sits in a hospice chair
watching the frames of his life unspool
like a spectator propped up upon a stool.

His once large appetites have all fled
into some dark recess inside his head
he eats when he is told to eat
he sleeps when he is told to sleep
he doesn't recall if he combed his hair
he forgot the time he fell down the stair.

He was once a big *macher* up on Chabanel
selling women's apparel to shops in Montréal
a born businessman, he wheeled and dealed
created a fashion empire almost without equal
was kind to shopkeepers and friends alike
loved his children and kept the menorah alight.

Now he hears only the thrum of a distant drummer
marvels at all the lost deals, all the lost summers
he watches the frames of his life unspool once again
and wonders at the loss of so many kin and friends
who would have thought this would be his last call
when time made spectators of us all.

Why is my City Changing So Fast?

A poem about a city remembered and a city new born

They spill out from trains and parking bays
propelled towards the urgencies of their day
commuters racing from the big train stations
their clear brows are furrowed by indiscretions
cellphones dangling like gold hoop earrings
they don't stop to see an old man like me
making his way downtown in a gray toupee.

It is a rushing blur of sight and sound
the glare of streetlights, the blare of horns
and syncopated neon in window shops
mixed with pungent smell of craft beer hops
my remembered old city has sunken down
beneath the excavations of this new town.
It's like I walk into a new city every day.

I used to ride the streetcar down to Peel
as it swayed slowly on its cold steel rails
secured to the road with cast iron nails
I would walk down to Dominion Square
to meet all the old timers loafing there
now it's all granite and aluminum stairs
and the harried commuters hardly care.

At noon I'd take lunch at Eaton's 9th floor
it was a magnificent place, all Art Deco
frescoes, vases and alabaster decor
I always ordered the special of the day
then washed it down with a little Chablis
now it has reopened in all its splendor
but it's way too pricey for me to enter.

Yes, my old city was once filled with fame
wolfing down smoked meat on the Main
watching the annual Stanley Cup parade
climbing the spiral stairs to shotgun houses
icing backyard hockey rinks from fire hoses
they have all disappeared in this new city
I have only one thing to say: What a pity!

I know this is all in the name of progressing
all the speed, the greed, but I am digressing
at the end of the day, I have one question to ask:

"Why is my city changing so fast?"

Whisperers of the Lachine Canal

A poem about a famous canal when river power was king

Bollard: a short, thick post on the deck of a ship or a quay to which a ship's rope may be secured.

The iron bollards whisper to me
as I bike along the Lachine Canal
strung out like black pearls along
the tanned arms of a debutante
they poke their bald eagle heads
out from the cracked stone quay.

They beseech me to free them
from where seamen tied hemp
rope around their thick necks
in service of demanding barons
who looked up and saw gold coins
sparkling on those still-pure waters.

The bollards murmur silent stories
of new factories and warehouses
reflected in the water of the canal
and communities bursting with Irish
come to build canals and new lives
as the Redpaths and Ogilvies grabbed
the brass ring, launching river freighters
and men to open trade and commerce
westward across this still-unborn nation.

The bollards charm me to peer deeply
into the opaque waters of the old canal
to reawaken the unrelenting cacophony
of loaded barges and river freighters
moving the currency of the day
iron ore, timber, textiles and sugar
through the locks towards the sea
extending the reach of Montréal
and ensuring its place in history.

The bollards whisper the faint cries
of women from blighted potato fields
they murmur the neighing of horses
straining to load steel and textiles
onto river barges for distant markets
they speak of the unending stream of
men and machines through iron locks
and of cursing foremen spurring on
weary labourers in the cold early dawn.

The Redpaths and Ogilvies are long gone
leaving only distant ghosts to bear witness
to the empires built from sweat and water
but the iron bollards have not forgotten
and the iron bollards have not forgiven
they stand like spent shells along the quay
silent for decades they still whisper to me
of times past when river power was king
and the Lachine Canal was the brass ring.

My Downtown Office Window

A poem about old men looking out of skyscraper windows

My downtown office window
looks out on Vieux-Montréal
luxury yachts and cruise ships
hurry by both large and small.

I peer through the glass and ask
"Where are all these folks going?"
if boating were my thing in life
I'd be in an old skiff just rowing.

Off to the far side of my window
rises a steel forest of rising towers
workers are buzzing up and down
building new condos in Griffentown.

If you look closely you might still find
traces of the tenements they replaced
the people in them look accusingly up
and obligingly disappear without a trace.

Near the Rivière St-Laurant, you can see
hollow flour mills and red-brick factories
almost all have now been fully restored
as artist studios and fancy jewelry stores.

If I had looked down a few years back
I'd have seen old sheds and railroad track
now the old sheds have all up and gone
and the railroad track has just moved on.

Up a little to the north lies our Mont Royal
a verdant mountain of old oaks and pine
it casts long shadows on the military graves
whose headstones are set out in perfect lines.

"Where will it all end?" I slowly ask myself
as I close the blinds against the late-day sun
it really doesn't matter come to think of it
because my days will soon all be but done.

The Newsstand Vendor

A poem about a forgotten institution swept off the street

He wanders the streets of
Vieux-Montréal
gnarled fingers around an
old ash cane
a blue Melton overcoat
across his thin cage.
does his head fall in regret or
in old age?

An oversized backpack
defeats his bent spine
impedes his step as he
recollects the old times
when his sidewalk newsstand
ruled rue St. Pierre
as he peddled La Presse, The
Gazette and l'Avenir.

To crooked politicians, celebrities and crooners
not to forget the ladies of a thousand nights
until la Ville de Montréal swept the newsstands
off the cobbled pavements and out of sight.

The tourists snap selfies and eat their poutine
he has seen it all before yet continues his routine
he's intent to walk the streets of his Vieux-Montreal
until he sees it one more time in the banks of snow.

As the day fades fast he walks up rue St. Paul
and suddenly the old newsstand vendor sees it all
his newsstand standing as through a glass darkly
broad sheets and trinkets gleaming ever so brightly
he struggles to pass it, only slightly remembered
as he buttons his coat against the cold December.

The Summer Quilt

A poem about summer memories preserved in a quilt

The moments of last summer
are falling too quickly down
from our old red maple tree
to the swiftly chilling ground.
Each leaf carries a memory
of those carefree summer days
a patchwork summer quilt
that settles lightly in the haze.

A summer quilt of broiling days
spent sweltering in the sun
followed by open terrace nights
with pungent smells of rum.
Then biking up a salty sweat
along a winding river bank
and gritty days at the beach
building castles in the sand.

I see these summer memories
each a bright red maple swath
in this lovely patchwork quilt
laying firmly across the earth.
But with the approaching snow
each memory will disappear
as we huddle in our cozy beds
waiting for spring to reappear.

When spring finally does arrive
around our old red maple tree
uncovering all the winter snow
with last summer's memories.
They'll shine for a brief moment
as we tumble in last year's leaves
then we'll look up and try to guess
all the new summer's memories.

Café les Deux Magots

A poem about a most famous café in Paris

It's Art Deco down to its very Saint-Germain core
they all hang out here, Verlaine,
Joyce, Jean-Paul
even Ernest Hemingway who sits at
his table
penning a tale of two debauched
Americanos
in post-war Paris, or so he boasts to
his friends.

Picasso has just met his Dora Maar
at the door.
will she become the love of his life, who knows?
He passes all day chatting her up with brioche
and cappuccino, leaving his blue genie to wait
above a barren canvas in his studio up the street.

Sartre can't get enough of the essence of this place
his angst pours out of the walls and onto the floor
along with cups of strong espresso that he sips
to keep from falling asleep with Simone by his seat
existentially, as he would no doubt have you know.

James paints portraits of artists as young men
writing on a narrow mahogany table at the rear
swearing he will publish a masterpiece next year
he babbles on in one unpunctuated wake and
cries for his Dublin days and his Irish poke cake.

One day the tourists will queue up for short espresso
basking in history as if they were Jake Barnes himself
and this was 1920s on the Boulevard Saint-Germain
I too will sip history with Americano, pining for the past
that they all saw reflected in the long-mirrored glass.

Heat Wave

A poem about the effects of heat on love remembered

It rose up yesterday a blast furnace of heat
cooking the dry cobblestone pavements
it reached into every pore and drew blood
a vampire grinning from the face of the sun.

This air hangs heavy at the base of my lungs
I slowly creep through the burning shadows
seeking a hidden fountain within a dark cave
where parched lips try to cry out to be saved.

The hot winds torch an exploding white sky
even the clouds seek shelter within the alleys
I pine for evening to come, to carry me away
to sing me to sleep in some blue alpine valley.

But it is the memory of you laying cool fingers
upon me, as the breeze through the lace curtains
gently strums the springs of our cast iron bed
that brings peace at last and cool dreams ahead.

It's Retirement Time

A poem about slipping silently into retirement

It's retirement time.
I've swept away
all the lost years
all the small fears
the insincerities
the peculiarities
swept them all away
into the cubby holes
of a rolltop desk.

I've watched it all
waft silently upward
like black smoke
above an angry fire
uncelebrated ghosts
of transparent dreams
slipping quietly through
a glass darkly.

The years have vanished
into old dusty ledgers
between aged books
and into self-reflection
leaving barely a trace
not even a distraction.

But it's retirement time.
I've posted the last bill
cut the last cheque
made the last deposit
closed the last drawer
and shut the last light.

And I wonder now
where it all went
and I wonder how
it got so damn spent
those unnamed years
those mundane fears
falling from etched brows
like summer rain tapping
against a windowpane.

But it's retirement time.
I will slam the glass door
turn the brass key
descend the rear stair
and slowly sail away
across a broad sea.

IV. Songs of Grace & Grief

Family, Legacy & Spiritual Reckoning

Here are poems of grace and grief whether found in a city railway station, in a man determined to go out in style or in the tragedy of another man in the decline of Alzheimer's.

These poems speak of a retired school teacher who treasures each one of her students of 38 years, how having grandchildren completes us, and about finding comfort after a child's death.

These poems sing of sorrow, remembrance and the grace that can rise out of loss.

Finding Grace at Windsor Station

A poem about a little girl and the true meaning of grace

A venerable old railway station
beating heart of the Canadian Pacific
it has graced Montreal since 1889
with its Romanesque Revival facade
rustic stonework, towers and turrets
impenetrable on thick rock footings
built to endure the shifting bedrock
of world wars and personal calamity.

As I walk through its glass-roofed main
hall
I hear the silence of those who came
before
I see the uncertain arms of hope reaching out
from eastern Europe, Asia, Italy and beyond.

I sense the first hope of boat-weary immigrants
desperate in gray rags from blighted fields abroad
I see the last hope on the faces of war-bound boys
stiff in gray wool enroute to the killing fields.

I feel the relief of lost souls newly found
and the fear of mothers for their lost sons
I see the first unsure kisses of new couples
and the last desperate kisses of young recruits
their sweethearts waving upwards reassuredly
from quickly disappearing railway platforms.

I smell the sulfur rising in thick black columns
from the iron bowels of steam locomotives
and the chug-a-chug of troop trains arriving
and departing to conquest and other glories.

I shiver beneath the wrought iron arches
and withdraw from the dank limestone walls
I marvel at the throngs of ever new arrivals
filling the great glass hall with the faint hope
they've crammed into ancient steamer trunks.

But hidden between all these storied pages
I cannot forget the simple joy of a foster child
who having just found an unexpected present
beneath the Christmas branches of a Scots Pine
tears open the present in tiny arms and beams
the sweet smile that swept slowly across her face
showed me the true meaning of finding grace.

Unveiling for My Son

A poem about the Jewish practice of unveiling a headstone

I stand beside my son's unmarked grave
where I'll unveil a headstone to his name
a simple inscription to mark his passing:
"Rest in peace my son, a peace everlasting."

He was three years old when taken away
it was last year on the first winter-cold day
as the snow fell across the barren ground
covering his grave without chancing a sound
where I wept as I waited for the coming spring
to unveil a headstone to his unmarked grave.

Now winter snow slinks down the drains
melted away by the soft spring rains
winter snow creeps off the gable tops
into the gutters and down the eave troughs
warm spring sun unveils the flowers
unveils the tulips along the bowers
unveils a scrabble cemetery ground
with dead leaves and puddles all around.

I will remove the cloth around his headstone
sweep away the dead leaves drain the puddles
and finally mark my son's untimely passing:
"Rest in peace my son, a peace everlasting."

Before the Last Solitude

A poem about going out in style

Before the last solitude
I shall live my days large
trade my old vintage coat
for something more bespoke
take a limo up to Park
nibble on scones and tea
at the old Queen E
savour truffles with cheese
then wash it all down
with a little Chablis.

Before the last solitude
I shall quit this old room
and fly boldly beyond
the boredom of my days
cry from a mountain peak
soar through a green valley
run on sore bony feet
along a sweet summer bank
savour the bitter perfume
of ripe red raspberries
after a soft spring rain.

Before the last solitude
I shall visit you once more
place those favourite lilies
across your shallow grave
recall the joy of your lips
grazing my smooth brow
and the sweet tenderness
of your parting embrace
then vanish into the sun
towards the last solitude.

At last.

Alzheimer's

A poem about the devastation caused by this disease

Every day brings me fewer memories, fewer thoughts
they shear away like tree bark from around my core
my trunk has become thinner, almost translucent
it refuses to support me, forces my limbs to droop.

My roots are starting to show, pushing out of the ground
and trying to strangle me where I'm bound to this chair
will I topple over into nothingness? Or sway in a storm?
colours linger beyond my focus, become black and white.

I do not know where I am; this place is an uninvited stranger
its four walls entrap me, do not let me see my spotted hands
or recall the touch of warm arms on long summer nights
sounds sink muffled like the death rattle of snakes in a pit.

I've lost my clothes and shudder in the frozen winter air
my fallen limbs are buried beneath the black winter snow
I don't feel any older but my hair hangs gray as cold soot
scattered on the ground around me by silent storms.

They tell me I've lived large, have grasped the brass ring
but when all is said and done I think no such thing
I have run out of questions I have run out of rhymes
I have survived another season but have lost my mind.

At the Last Trumpet Call

A poem about self-doubt and salvation

I worked tirelessly, loved selflessly
helped willingly, lost graciously
saved carefully, waved patriotically.

But at the last trumpet call
will it have been worth it after all?

I donated frequently, planned carefully
dreamed happily, schemed harmlessly
forgave blamelessly, cried shamelessly.

But at the last trumpet call
will I have been saved from the fall?

Now I can hear it, the last trumpet call
sounding its last note, I will not fear it
it will come for me in the still of the night
intending to take me away in its sure flight.

But I will not run from it, I will not hide from it
with the arms of a lover I will surely embrace it
when the last trumpet call has finally sounded
I will vanish into a sleep, a sleep unbounded.

Students of 38 Years

A poem about dedication and retirement

As she finally closes her classroom door
whiteboards wiped, books piled, little chairs
stacked and staring back empty and mute
she recalls each of her students of 38 years
they pass so vividly across her still-clear brow
staring up shyly from her once-open door.

She has shaped each of her students of 38 years
showed them a glimpse of worlds yet unseen
shared the awe rising in their new-child smiles
as they learned how to read, write and dare
tried to wake in each student a spark of fire
to ignite an explosion of wonder in their eyes.

She has loved each of her students of 38 years
she nurtured them tenderly in her open arms
until they were ready to soar up and fly
take on the world if that was their calling
on the rising updraft of her generous heart
now broken as the door finally slams shut.

The Concertina Man

A poem about playing old time tunes in the street

There he sits on the cobblestones
playing familiar tunes all afternoon
some would say his playing is bad
his songs are happy until they're sad.

His calloused hands move air in and
out
as they push the jigs and polkas all
about
but no one's listening on this
afternoon
they've got other things they have to
do.

Greensleeves, Family Jig, polkas
galore
the tunes just keep coming evermore
tourists rush by with their kids in tow
as the concertina man plays Keel Row.

But the concertina man does not relent
he plays his tunes until the day is spent
then packs his instrument safely away
he'll surely be back the following day.

Our Unmarked Graves

A poem about forgotten soldiers in unmarked graves

We are the unknown soldiers
lying beneath fields of stone
under a gray gun-metal sky
the piercing morning sun
only unveils the barren ground
above our unmarked graves.

We cannot break out
of this soundless crypt
where lost lovers cry out
to their long-lost braves
now all unknown soldiers
in their unmarked graves.

We too have felt the bliss
of a lover's cool fingertips
across our smooth brows
then watched death creep
in bullets of darkening shadow
across our unmarked graves.

Will we ever be heard again
above the lost battle fray?
Will we ever be held again by
downy arms on summer days?
Or, are we condemned to lie
forever in our unmarked graves?

The Fallen Men

A poem in tribute to T.S. Eliot

We are the fallen men
forever trapped beneath
this unyielding dark sea
we lurk in black shadow
fragile as thin coral reef
lashed by rogue waves
though we pray for rescue
no one hears our call
though we pray for mercy
no one sees our fall
trapped in a watery grave
we are left to curl thinly
like gossamer smoke
dancing ever upwards
from smoldering fires.

We are the fallen men
entombed in old ships,
skuttled by buccaneers
in uncharted seas
we glance up to the light
but no one can see us
we listen into the night
but no one can hear us
the angry ocean surge
mutes our faint calls
like a grinning clown
it mocks our fall.

We are the fallen men
hidden in the decaying
shells of sunken ships
we lie here forgotten
despite all of our pleas
we try to unshackle
these ropes to be free
our children's last fears
can't even reach us
our lovers' last tears
can't even cheat us.

Are we to live forever
in this watery grave?
Are we to call forever
for us to be saved?
Or shall we rise up
on unexpected wings
soar ever upwards
and find a new way?
Find salvation again
at the end of the day?

Go Ask the Generals

A poem about war and the silence of generals

When beneath
the blood-red sky
the battle-sun has set
and voices are stilled
by fear and night
go ask the Generals
if the war was right.

Go ask the Generals
if *they* fought and fell
where strategy marked
their perfect graves
or if deeds undone
cheated fate and left
a thousand hearts unclaimed.

Where lips call no more
to lovers dimmed by time
and brave boy-eyes
that once held destiny
stare glassy in the night
go ask the Generals
if the war was right.

Go ask the Generals
if dawn pinned honour
to their hollow breasts
or if false victories
filled their mouths
with lead and left
a thousand silenced cries.

When the battle dies
like an unfinished tear
on a young boy's cheek
cold and laid out
in a grave of night
go ask the Generals
if the war was right.

Stone Steps to God

A poem about taking comfort where it is found

They climb the stone steps to God
she hoping to find some comfort
after the death of their infant son
he not so sure deliverance is waiting
at the top of the curved stone climb.

Hand in hand they struggle upwards
she will kneel down before the altar
and pray for the soul of their child
he will kneel down as well, more to
ease her soul than that of his son.

They will both look upward in awe
toward the breathtaking arched
dome
and take some solace in its ethereal
light
burning through the stained glass walls
as it unveils the face of their lost child.

Then they will descend the stone steps
to return to the basement of their days
they will leave the embrace of the light
and back to the numbness of their ways
each taking comfort where it is found.

V. Meaning in a Changing World

Fate, Fear & Meaning

The journey is nearing its end with poems speaking of existence and a longing for meaning.

These poems ask, "Who pulls the strings? What lies between two moments?"

They probe the mysteries of existence and the expectations of a lost generation.

With dark staging and questioning of our very being, they echo fears we rarely name aloud and dare us to confront our invisible choreographers.

Lost Generation

A poem about the trials and tribulations of being a baby boomer

We were the last great hope of a lost generation
risen from the sad song of mothers for lost sons
across distant battlefields long forgotten and gone.

We entered life with smiles of hope and heart
conceived to mute the battle cries of lost grief
they coddled us like no other generation before.

Expectations for us were set so impossibly high
we were born for failure before our first breath
and in the end, couldn't even quite accomplish that.

We entered a world scarred by the bullets of war
we sowed hope where hope had long ceased to be
cried out with silver spoons in our infant mouths.

Beneath the weight of so much hope and heart
we measured out the meaning of our morning lives
with coffee spoons, as that famous poet once said.

We have long climbed out from those shallow graves
known success as no other generation has before
raised our own children but never fully ourselves.

Now we turn away from those distant battlefields
from those mothers who still call for their lost sons
we will never stoop to join their sad swan songs
we will not feel their pain, will not hear their cries
for we have turned back the hands of time.

Eyes Wide Shut

A poem about phone jocks on a commuter train

I see them most every other office day
taking the 7:52 down to Lucien L'Alliée
a whole commuter car of downtown jocks
chins way down to their bespoke socks
with eyes laser focused upon their phones
they are tightly packed but completely alone.

Their manicured fingers move robotically
across the tiny squares of their virtual keys
they can't see beyond their iPhone screens
they can only hope to remain mostly unseen
as their ringed fingers scroll, sweep and tap
another urgent TikTok video about their cat.

I stare at them more than I probably should
try to read their faces beneath their hoods
but they seldom look up to see who's there
and truth be told, I don't think they care
they barely wiggle in their red vinyl seats
I have to giggle at their immaculate pleats.

When we arrive at the terminal train station
they're all off without a moment's hesitation
cell phones clutched in leather-gloved hands
along with leather satchels and rubber bands
I have to wonder where they're all going
as for me, I'm pleased to do a little trolling.

Caught Between Two Moments

A poem about what lies between two moments in time

They rest peaceably in
the old farmer's field
the worn tractor tires
retired from the wheel
the snow provides
shelter on cold winter
days
and fall leaves colour
them in intricate ways
spring lifts their heads from out of the frost
and hot summer days leave them all but lost.

But what's up with that strange one there
you know, the one seeming to defy the air?
Insisting on standing its ground on the right
reluctant to go quietly into that good night.

Caught in uncertainty between two moments
not quite face down nor ready for atonement
while it leans precariously in this unlikely state
we are left waiting for time to decide its fate.

Will it keel over like a headstone in the grass
or stand full up and roll down a country path?
These mysteries are seemingly too hard to explain
caught between two moments lies the beauty and pain.

Café du Port

A poem about a little café in Vieux-Montréal

Out from their Ubers stroll the
beautiful people
on Prada stilettos with Coco
Chanel smiles
their tanned arms hail friends
with perfect form
enameled fingers clutching their
Vuitton bags
as they meet at the Café du Port
for evening drinks
to chat and gossip away the long
summer night
with crystal stemmed glasses of
Château Lafite.

A hidden jewel in Vieux-
Montréal, the Café du Port
spills onto a minor street that smells of Paris
but thankfully without the attitude or tariffs
a stone's throw from rue St. Paul where
harried tourists listen to the concertina man
play polkas and jigs for any spare change
and partake of our national cuisine, la poutine.

But the beautiful people are just happy to chat
recall the day's indiscretions, the minor obsessions
gossip about that new hot series on Apple TV
run out the clock with more glasses of Chablis
formulate intrigues for the new autumn season
then call it a night for no apparent reason.

As the beautiful people leave the Café du Port
swathed in a summer breeze reassuringly perfect
for blowing smoke rings into the midnight sky
they disappear into their pre-arranged rides
then home to aluminum and concrete towers
to dream of lost lovers and indiscreet flowers.

The Mad Puppeteer

A poem about who is actually pulling the strings

We are pulled and danced in a contorted mirror
arms and legs controlled by a mad puppeteer
like puppets trapped on a forbidden stage
our strings pulled by some fiendish sage
we are caught in this unknown place and time
moving towards an end without reason or rhyme.

The puppeteer commands us to perform our dance
the theatre lights blind us, we do not have a chance
we can only observe where we currently stand
as for what lies ahead it's just a line in the sand
we don't know how long this spectacle will last
we can only guess our future and forget our past.

But we will soon disappear from this puppet stage
turned away by the puppeteer's capricious rage
we will leave this life and throw off these strings
as the mad puppeteer laughs and cuts our wings
then at last we will descend sweetly into a sleep
where devils fear to tread and angels weep.

The Nature of Rivers

A poem about the true nature of rivers

"Rivers remember voices, someone's name, a guilt."

- Michael Ondaatje

Rivers don't run straight down to the sea
they meander like a shamefaced lover
caught in the throes of some duplicitous act.

They babble on like a gray man with a cane
telling tall tales to expectant grandchildren
they carry muted voices from mountain ice
and amplify them in the wet arms of the ocean.

They bury guilt in their sandbank twists and turns
and show only the shear smooth surface of things.

They murmur out the names of unnamed explorers
who have tried to ford them in birchbark canoes.

They confirm the past and warn us of the future.

The Last Judgement at Chartres

A poem about the Judge of humanity at the famous cathedral

Grey thin ghost of Calvary hill
fixed for all time in coloured glass
you stare out with fragile immobility
a sad court jester from the past
bound in lead.

The morning light ignites your eyes
unshrouds the apostles at your feet
their robes ablaze in red and blue
they ask only one simple question:
Are we the judges or your
salvation?

As the sun rises slowly to its peak
it steals the certainty in your eyes
which in the noon light roll out
upon the scattered pages of time
and slowly weep.

With dusk approaching from the west
throwing dark shadow across your face
it steals your holy crown of thorns
concealing the magic of your charms
that dawn light revealed in the glass.

Now angels blow the trumpet call
to announce the end of days for all
with Saint Michael weighing rise or fall
as shrouded bodies await their fate
and devils drive sinners down the hall.

Finally, the soft light of the setting sun
marks the end of days the end has come
as the arch angels try to read your face
their mouths of glass cry out for grace
I too will surrender to your power
this the beauty of my hour.

VI. Poetry Through a Rearview Mirror

Ghosts, Treehouses & Rearview Mirrors

The end of the journey sees us heading homeward, not just to physical locations, but to emotional ones as well. These poems visit places, sensations and memories with a tender touch.

Whether viewed through the wheelhouse of a haunted tugboat or through the window of a bedridden patient, they offer closure with just enough ambiguity to feel true.

Closing on resolution and renewal, this endpiece celebrates life through the frame of a rearview mirror turned around to peer into what lies ahead.

Playhouse in the Trees

A poem about building a playhouse for the grandkids

The smell of just-sawed pine is magical
it gusts upward in the early August air
from the cold steel of my rusty saw
as I measure and cut the wide boards
for a new playhouse high in the trees
square and strong with a gabled roof
it rises from the hard scrabble ground
almost hiding in the crown of leaves.

I take special care with the anchors
making them strong, sure and secure
to cradle my future grandchildren
playing so high on the steady boughs
of our hundred year red maple tree
as they are lifted up to the entry hearth
in the unsure arms of our own children
to see where their grandma and grandpa
loved their grandchildren even more.

I see them playing now within its walls
scaring off imaginary hunters prowling
with rifles in arms on horses far below
watch them wondering at who made
such a grand hiding place in the forest.

But will they even suspect it was me
armed with rusty saws and hammers
who fashioned this with his bare hands
from dry sticks of wood and old nails?

Never mind, I will build it to last forever
I will build it for my future grandchildren
I will measure and cut and measure again
I will weave it into a gentle song to them
I see them now in their childhood delight
playing so high in the new morning light.

The Ghosts of the Daniel McAllister

A poem about the rebirth of a grande dame

OMG!

I see her ghosts in the
wheelhouse now
setting a course for some long
lost glory
when the Daniel McAllister
was the king
of ocean-going boats and old
salt stories.

The poor tug sits on a concrete cradle
at a rusting bollard on a deserted dock
serving only as an unwilling diversion
for TikToc tourists and YouTube jocks.

In a sad testament to those glory days
she's leaking water from her rotting keel
like an abondoned geriatric grande dame
strapped to a hospice bed beside a wheel.

But the ghosts of the Daniel McAllister
will not suffer the disgrace of this end
they will smell the deisel on the wind
and feel her keel shudder once again.

And now they have really retaken the wheel!
I can see their churlish grins atop her mast
they are readying to set off one last time
to journey back into some forgotten past.

Yes, the ghosts of the Daniel McAllister
call to me from their wind-lashed throne
they'll be departing this grave at any time
and casting off for parts unknown.

My Magic Bedroom Window

A poem about how a bedroom window frames a masterpiece

My magic bedroom window frames
a masterpiece of low hills and trees
I think of it as my fine art museum
displaying new paintings each season.

Though I am now bound to this room
my eyes see clearly what lies outside
I marvel at how each new masterpiece
is framed in my window as I peer outside.

In spring, my magic bedroom window
wakes me just before first hint of dawn
with the song of young sparrows and jays
and the fresh dew laced across the lawn.

My window frames the ruins of snow
stealing down from peaks above the hill
it reveals the small red maple saplings
coming alive in the early-morning chill.

In summer, my magic bedroom window
frames a tall stand of mixed elm and pine
a dancing collage in vivid stabs of green
hiding an unanswered question in rhyme.

And just up on a distant and hazy ridge
framed by a line of white-clad birch
I can see an ivy red-bricked belfry
atop a deserted Methodist church.

In fall, my magic bedroom window
paints a Matisse for my failing eyes
orange and red slashes of pigment
come alive on the wood fence stile.

As I marvel at this burst of colour
I ask myself from my narrow bed:
Will I ever be able to feel its grace?
Will I ever touch its charmed face?

In winter, my magic bedroom window
frames only an empty mask of frost
it steals the portraits from my sight
even the elm and pine trees are lost.

Try as I might I cannot see anything
beyond the lines in the cold glass lite
even the ivy-bricked belfry is gone:
Was it stolen during a chilly night?

But of all the splendid masterpieces
my magic bedroom window frames
spring, summer, autumn or winter
in the end they're all the same.

And in the uncertainty of my final days
I'm certain nothing will surpass the sight
of my window framing your sweet face
as you climb the porch to warm my night.

Our Children's Children

A poem about how having grandchildren completes us

They are racing through the evening grass
our children's children
as we sit and watch their raucous play
an amazing churn of arms and legs
it punctuates our remaining days
like bookends on an unread shelf.

They are bathing now in the soaker tub
our children's children
captaining pirate ships on soapy seas
swimming beneath the bubbly swell
then pulling the plug in wonderment
as an ocean vanishes down the drain.

They are listening now to storytime
our children's children
limbs gathered askew on the couch
staring with eyes wide and fixed
as we read them dark tales
of big bad wolves and magic tricks.

They are sleeping soundly in their beds
our children's children
their gentle breathing
whispers a confirmation
from beneath the bedroom door
finally, music to our ears.

It completes us.

Life Through a Rearview Mirror

A poem about viewing the future in a rearview mirror

I was always looking into my rearview mirror
obsessed with what I saw was happening there
I needed to relive all the mislaid chances
the crazy romances, the suspect glances
my world was based upon one false premise:
that the view in my mirror was a constant menace.

Now I've turned my rearview mirror around
it faces what lies ahead, around each new bend
instead of the drumbeat of a past life undone
I've set my mirror towards a life yet to come
it reflects the future like a turning crystal ball
tossed by a blind toddler down an unlit hall.

I rise each morning with a new sense of gravity
my mirror reflects a world of untold possibilities
it removes the veils that once completely covered
what I had yet to see, what I had yet to discover
the menace in my mirror has now been replaced
by a beacon of light that reflects a new face.

It's certain that my future will one day be done
I'll reach the end of this road, the end of the run
my rearview mirror will stare back at me darkly
offer me no more insights then ask me starkly:
"Do you really want to know what lies ahead?"
as I ponder the question and crawl back to bed.

Closing Reflections

Life is not measured perfectly along a timeline but by the moments in life's journey that shape us, the questions unanswered, the lovers remembered and lost, the windows that frame each season with new meaning. *Poetry Through a Rearview Mirror* traces such moments across a lifetime, gathering them not as isolated events but as reflections seen through a rearview mirror.

The poems here whisper of April mornings and unanswered prayers, of losses that tremble quietly behind closed doors and of everyday miracles that flicker in the eyes of our children's children. They do not claim certainty, but they claim beauty, grace and the kind of tenderness that survives cynicism.

If there is one abiding message in these pages it is that life is composed of fleeting harmonies between joy and sorrow, memory and forgetting, and in honoring these harmonies, we find our truest songs.

Thank you for joining me on this journey.

Gordon J. Mitchell – Montréal, Québec
October 2025